Light Cooking™

CHICKEN

PUBLICATIONS INTERNATIONAL, LTD.

Recipe Development: Sue Spitler, Food Consultant, Incredible Edibles, Ltd.
Nutritional Analysis: Linda R. Yoakam, M.S., R.D.

Food Guide Pyramid source: U.S. Department of Agriculture/U.S. Department of Health and Human Services.

Photography on page 87 by Sacco Productions Limited, Chicago. Cover and remaining photography by Burke/Triolo Productions, Culver City, CA.

Pictured on the front cover: Chicken Baked in Parchment *(page 90)*.

Pictured on the back cover *(from top to bottom)*: Mediterranean Chicken Kabobs *(page 84)*, Mexican Tortilla Soup *(page 50)*, Tarragon Chicken Salad Sandwiches *(page 20)* and Szechuan Chicken Salad *(page 38)*.

Pictured on the inside front cover: Mediterranean Sandwiches *(page 18)*.

Pictured on the inside back cover: Tuscan Chicken Breasts with Polenta *(page 81)*.

ISBN: 0-7853-0784-2

Manufactured in U.S.A.

8 7 6 5 4 3 2 1

CONTENTS

Lessons in Smart Eating ——————————— 6

Sandwiches & Snacks ——————————— 12

Salads ——————————— 28

Soups & Stews ——————————— 42

Entrees ——————————— 58

Nutrition Reference Chart ——————————— 92

Index ——————————— 93

LESSONS IN SMART EATING

Today, people everywhere are more aware than ever before about the importance of maintaining a healthful lifestyle. In addition to proper exercise, this includes eating foods that are lower in fat, sodium and cholesterol. The goal of *Light Cooking* is to provide today's cook with easy-to-prepare recipes that taste great, yet easily fit into your dietary goals. Eating well is a matter of making smarter choices about the foods you eat. Preparing the recipes in *Light Cooking* is your first step toward making smart choices a delicious reality.

A Balanced Diet

The U.S. Department of Agriculture and the Department of Health and Human Services has developed a Food Guide Pyramid to illustrate how easy it is to eat a healthier diet. It is not a rigid prescription, but rather a general guide that lets you choose a healthful diet that's right for you. It calls for eating a wide variety of foods to get the nutrients you need and, at the same time, the right amount of calories to maintain a healthy weight.

Food Guide Pyramid
A Guide to Daily Food Choices

Fats, Oils, & Sweets
Use Sparingly
(Also found in other groups; see text.)

KEY
•Fat (naturally occurring and added)   ▾Sugar (added)
These symbols show fats, oils, and added sugars in foods.

Milk, Yogurt, & Cheese Group
2–3 Servings

Meat, Poultry, Fish, Dry Beans, Eggs, & Nuts Group
2–3 Servings

Vegetable Group
3–5 Servings

Fruit Group
2–4 Servings

Bread, Cereal, Rice, & Pasta Group
6–11 Servings

The number of servings, and consequently, the number of calories a person can eat each day, is determined by a number of factors, including age, weight, height, activity level and gender. Sedentary women and some older adults need about 1,600 calories each day. For most children, teenage girls, active women and many sedentary men 2,000 calories is about right. Teenage boys, active men and some very active women use about 2,800 calories each day. Use the chart below to determine how many servings you need for your calorie level.

Personalized Food Group Servings for Different Calorie Levels*			
	1,600	2,000	2,800
Bread Group Servings	6	8	11
Vegetable Group Servings	3	4	5
Fruit Group Servings	2	3	4
Milk Group Servings	2-3**	2-3**	2-3**
Meat Group Servings (ounces)	5	6	7

* Numbers may be rounded.
** Women who are pregnant or breast-feeding, teenagers and young adults to age 24 need 3 or more servings.

Lower Fat for Healthier Living

It is widely known that most Americans' diets are too high in fat. A low fat diet reduces your risk of getting certain diseases and helps you maintain a healthy weight. Studies have shown that eating more than the recommended amount of fat (especially saturated fat) is associated with increased blood cholesterol levels in some adults. A high blood cholesterol level is associated with increased risk for heart disease. A high fat diet may also increase your chances for obesity and some types of cancer.

Nutrition experts recommend diets that contain 30% or less of total daily calories from fat. The "30% calories from fat" goal applies to a total diet over time, not to a single food, serving of a recipe or meal. To find the approximate percentage of calories from fat use this easy 3-step process:

1 Multiply the grams of fat per serving by 9 (there are 9 calories in each gram of fat), to give you the number of calories from fat per serving.

2 Divide by the total number of calories per serving.

3 Multiply by 100%.

For example, imagine a 200 calorie sandwich that has 10 grams of fat.
To find the percentage of calories from fat, first multiply the grams of fat by 9:

$$10 \times 9 = 90$$

Then, divide by the total number of calories in a serving:

$$90 \div 200 = .45$$

Multiply by 100% to get the percentage of calories from fat:

$$.45 \times 100\% = 45\%$$

You may find doing all this math tiresome, so an easier way to keep track of the fat in your diet is to calculate the total *grams* of fat appropriate to your caloric intake, then keep a running count of fat grams over the course of a day. The Nutrition Reference Chart on page 92 lists recommended daily fat intakes based on calorie level.

Defining "Fat Free"

It is important to take the time to read food labels carefully. For example, you'll find many food products on the grocery store shelves making claims such as "97% fat free." This does not necessarily mean that 97% of the *calories* are free from fat (or that only 3 percent of calories come from fat). Often these numbers are calculated by weight. This means that out of 100 grams of this food, 3 grams are fat. Depending on what else is in the food, the percentage of calories from fat can be quite high. You may find that the percent of calories *from fat* can be as high as 50%.

Daily Values

Fat has become the focus of many diets and eating plans. This is because most Americans' diets are too high in fat. However, there are other important nutrients to be aware of, including saturated fat, sodium, cholesterol, protein, carbohydrates and several vitamins and minerals. Daily values for these nutrients have been established by the government and reflect current nutritional recommendations for a 2,000 calorie reference diet. They are appropriate for most adults and children (age 4 or older) and provide excellent guidelines for an overall healthy diet. The chart on page 92 gives the daily values for 11 different items.

Nutritional Analysis

Every recipe in *Light Cooking* is followed by a nutritional analysis block that lists certain nutrient values for a single serving.

■   The analysis of each recipe includes all the ingredients that are listed in that recipe, *except* ingredients labeled as "optional" or "for garnish."

■   If a range is given in the yield of a recipe ("Makes 6 to 8 servings" for example), the *lower* yield was used to calculate the per serving information.

■   If a range is offered for an ingredient ("¼ to ⅛ teaspoon" for example), the *first* amount given was used to calculate the nutrition information.

■   If an ingredient is presented with an option ("2 cups hot cooked rice or noodles" for example), the *first* item listed was used to calculate the nutritional information.

■   Foods shown in photographs on the same serving plate and offered as "serve with" suggestions at the end of a recipe are *not* included in the recipe analysis unless they are listed in the ingredient list.

■   Meat should be trimmed of all visible fat since this is reflected in the nutritional analysis.

■   In recipes calling for cooked rice or noodles, the analysis was based on rice or noodles that were prepared without added salt or fat unless otherwise mentioned in the recipe.

■   All recipes that call for "vegetable oil" have been calculated using the values for canola oil.

■   Recipes in this publication call for "defatted broth." To defat broth, simply chill the canned broth thoroughly. Open the can and use a spoon to lift out any solid fat floating on the surface of the broth.

The nutrition information that appears with each recipe was calculated by an independent nutrition consulting firm. Every effort has been made to check the accuracy of these numbers. However, because numerous variables account for a wide range of values in certain foods, all analyses that appear in this book should be considered approximate.

The recipes in this publication are *not* intended as a medically therapeutic program, nor as a substitute for medically approved diet plans for people on fat, cholesterol or sodium restricted diets. You should consult your physician before beginning any diet plan. The recipes offered here can be a part of a healthy lifestyle that meets recognized dietary guidelines. A healthy lifestyle includes not only eating a balanced diet, but engaging in proper exercise as well.

All the ingredients called for in these recipes are generally available in large supermarkets, so there is no need to go to specialty or health food stores. You'll also see an ever-increasing amount of reduced fat and nonfat products available in local markets. Take advantage of these items to reduce your daily fat intake even more.

Cooking Healthier

When cooking great-tasting low fat meals, you will find some techniques or ingredients are different from traditional cooking. Fat serves as a flavor enhancer and gives foods a distinctive and desirable texture. In order to compensate for the lack of fat and still give great-tasting results, many of the *Light Cooking* recipes call for a selection of herbs or a combination of fresh vegetables. A wide variety of grains and pastas are also used. Many of the recipes call for alternative protein sources, such as dried beans or tofu. Often meat is included in a recipe as an accent flavor rather than the star attraction. Vegetables are often "sautéed" in a small amount of broth rather than oil. Applesauce may be added to baked goods to give a texture similar to full fat foods. These are all simple changes that you can easily make when you start cooking healthy!

Chicken—Helpful Hints

Chicken is a mainstay in the American diet. And now, more than ever before, it is appearing at meals with increasing frequency. Low in fat, calories and price, chicken has a universal taste appeal that can't be beat. It is also extremely versatile, lending itself to almost every type of cooking.

■ Check the package for the U.S.D.A. Grade A rating; chicken in most supermarkets should be government inspected. Look for secure, unbroken packaging, as well as a "sell-by" date stamp that indicates the last day the chicken should be sold.

■ Physically inspect the chicken before purchasing. Its skin should be creamy white to deep yellow; meat should never look gray or pasty. Odors could signal spoilage. If you notice a strong, unpleasant odor after opening a package of chicken, leave it open on the counter for a few minutes. Sometimes oxidation takes place inside the package, resulting in a slight, but harmless odor. If the odor remains, return the chicken in its original package to the store for a refund.

■   Fresh, raw chicken can be stored in its original wrap for up to two days in the coldest part of the refrigerator. However, freeze chicken immediately if you do not plan to use it within two days after purchasing. You can freeze most chicken in its original packaging safely for up to two months; if you plan to freeze it longer, consider double-wrapping or rewrapping with freezer paper, aluminum foil or plastic wrap. Airtight packaging is the key to freezing chicken successfully.

■   When freezing whole chickens, remove and rinse giblets (if any) and pat dry with paper towels. Trim away any excess fat from chicken. Tightly wrap, label, date and freeze both chicken and giblets in separate freezer-strength plastic, paper or foil wraps.

■   Thaw frozen chicken, wrapped, in the refrigerator for best results. Thawing times for frozen chicken vary depending on how thoroughly frozen the chicken is and whether the chicken is whole or cut up. A general guideline is to allow 24 hours thawing time for a 5-pound whole chicken; allow about 5 hours per pound for thawing chicken pieces. Never thaw chicken at room temperature; this promotes bacterial growth.

■   To save money, purchase whole chickens on sale and cut them apart at home. Save time by stocking the freezer with ready-to-use boneless skinless chicken. Store the chicken in efficient, meal-size portions; they defrost and cook quickly and eliminate leftovers. Two whole chicken breasts (about 12 ounces each) yield about 2 cups chopped cooked chicken. One broiler-fryer (about 3 pounds) yields about 2½ cups chopped cooked chicken.

Handling Chicken

■   When handling raw chicken, you must keep everything that comes into contact with it clean. Raw chicken should be rinsed and patted dry with paper towels before cooking; cutting boards and knives must be washed in hot sudsy water after using and hands must be scrubbed thoroughly before and after handling. Why? Raw chicken can harbor harmful salmonella bacteria. If bacteria are transferred to work surfaces, utensils or hands, they could contaminate other foods as well as the cooked chicken and cause food poisoning. With careful handling and proper cooking, this is easily prevented.

■   Chicken should always be cooked completely before eating. You should never cook chicken partially, then store it to be finished later, since this promotes bacterial growth as well.

■   To determine if a whole chicken is thoroughly cooked, a meat thermometer inserted into the thickest part of the thigh, but not near the bone or fat, should register 180° to 185°F. To test bone-in chicken pieces, you should be able to insert a fork into the chicken with ease and the juices should run clear. Boneless chicken pieces are done when the centers are no longer pink.

SANDWICHES & SNACKS

THE CALIFORNIAN

❖

Alfalfa sprouts add a delicate nutty flavor plus crunchy goodness to these open-faced sandwiches. Sprouts are low in calories and fat free. Purchase sprouts that are moist and crisp; refrigerate and use within a few days of purchase.

❖

3 tablespoons reduced fat cream cheese, softened
1 tablespoon chutney
4 slices pumpernickel bread
4 lettuce leaves
¾ pound thinly sliced chicken breast (from deli)
1⅓ cups alfalfa sprouts
1 medium mango, peeled and sliced
1 pear, cored and sliced
4 strawberries

1 Combine cream cheese and chutney in small bowl; spread about 1 tablespoon on each bread slice. Place 1 lettuce leaf over cream cheese mixture. Divide chicken evenly; place over lettuce.

2 Arrange alfalfa sprouts over chicken; arrange mango and pear slices over sprouts. Garnish each open-faced sandwich with a strawberry.

Makes 4 servings

Nutrients per Serving:

Calories	318
(17% of calories from fat)	
Total Fat	6 g
Saturated Fat	2 g
Cholesterol	72 mg
Sodium	304 mg
Carbohydrate	36 g
Dietary Fiber	6 g
Protein	30 g
Calcium	69 mg
Iron	2 mg
Vitamin A	239 RE
Vitamin C	45 mg

DIETARY EXCHANGES:
1 Starch/Bread, 3 Lean Meat, 1½ Fruit

❖

Cook's Tip

To easily peel and slice a mango, simply place the fruit on a cutting board with one of the ends pointing toward you. Slice vertically down either side of the pit. Use a paring knife to remove the peel from the fruit. Cut the fruit away from the pit; then, cut the fruit into slices.

❖

GRILLED CHICKEN BREAST AND PEPERONATA SANDWICHES

❖

Peperonata is an Italian mixture of sweet peppers, onions and garlic cooked in olive oil. Look for peppers that are firm, thick-fleshed and bright in color. Peppers contain twice as much vitamin C as oranges and are high in vitamin A and fiber. One-half cup of raw pieces contains only 14 calories.

❖

1 tablespoon olive oil or vegetable oil
1 medium red bell pepper, sliced into strips
1 medium green bell pepper, sliced into strips
¾ cup onion slices (about 1 medium)
2 cloves garlic, minced
¼ teaspoon salt
¼ teaspoon black pepper
4 boneless skinless chicken breast halves (about 1 pound)
4 small French rolls, split and toasted

1 Heat oil in large nonstick skillet over medium heat until hot. Add bell peppers, onion and garlic; cook and stir 5 minutes. Reduce heat to low; cook and stir about 20 minutes or until vegetables are very soft. Sprinkle with salt and black pepper.

2 Grill chicken, on covered grill over medium-hot coals, 10 minutes on each side or until chicken is no longer pink in center. Or, broil chicken, 6 inches from heat source, 7 to 8 minutes on each side or until chicken is no longer pink in center.

3 Place chicken in rolls. Divide pepper mixture evenly; spoon over chicken.

Makes 4 servings

Nutrients per Serving:

Calories	321
(22% of calories from fat)	
Total Fat	8 g
Saturated Fat	2 g
Cholesterol	58 mg
Sodium	497 mg
Carbohydrate	36 g
Dietary Fiber	3 g
Protein	27 g
Calcium	48 mg
Iron	2 mg
Vitamin A	28 RE
Vitamin C	36 mg

DIETARY EXCHANGES:
2 Starch/Bread, 2½ Lean Meat, 1½ Vegetable

❖

Cook's Tip
Using a skillet with a nonstick finish lets you cook food without sticking while using much less oil or margarine. Most nonstick finishes are dishwasher safe, but remember to use nonmetal utensils while cooking to prevent scratching the surface.

❖

BUFFALO CHICKEN TENDERS

With just a few easy changes, this favorite appetizer is updated to fit into today's healthy eating plan. Chicken tenders are marinated in hot sauce and then baked, rather than fried, in this low fat version. Cool off these spicy chicken chunks by dunking them in a low fat blue cheese dressing.

3 tablespoons Louisiana-style hot sauce
½ teaspoon paprika
¼ teaspoon ground red pepper
1 pound chicken tenders
½ cup fat free blue cheese dressing
¼ cup reduced fat sour cream
2 tablespoons crumbled blue cheese
1 medium red bell pepper, cut into ½-inch slices

1 Preheat oven to 375°F. Combine hot sauce, paprika and ground red pepper in small bowl; brush on all surfaces of chicken. Place chicken in greased 11 × 7-inch baking pan. Cover; marinate in refrigerator 30 minutes.

2 Bake, uncovered, about 15 minutes or until chicken is no longer pink in center.

3 Combine blue cheese dressing, sour cream and blue cheese in small serving bowl. Garnish as desired. Serve with chicken and bell pepper for dipping.

Makes 10 servings

Nutrients per Serving:

Calories	83
(27% of calories from fat)	
Total Fat	2 g
Saturated Fat	1 g
Cholesterol	27 mg
Sodium	180 mg
Carbohydrate	5 g
Dietary Fiber	0 g
Protein	9 g
Calcium	14 mg
Iron	<1 mg
Vitamin A	19 RE
Vitamin C	7 mg

DIETARY EXCHANGES:
½ Starch/Bread, 1 Lean Meat

Health Note

Eating hot and spicy foods may actually be beneficial! Capsaicinoids, which are what actually produce the burning sensation in the mouth, work as anticoagulants, possibly helping to prevent heart attacks or strokes caused by blood clots.

MEDITERRANEAN SANDWICHES

   Nonstick cooking spray
1¼ pounds chicken tenders, cut crosswise in half
 1 large tomato, cut into bite-size pieces
 ½ small cucumber, seeded and sliced
 ½ cup sweet onion slices (about 1 small)
 2 tablespoons cider vinegar
 1 tablespoon olive oil or vegetable oil
 3 teaspoons minced fresh oregano *or* ½ teaspoon dried oregano leaves
 2 teaspoons minced fresh mint *or* ½ teaspoon dried mint leaves
 ¼ teaspoon salt
12 lettuce leaves (optional)
 6 whole wheat pita breads, cut crosswise in half

1 Spray large nonstick skillet with cooking spray; heat over medium heat until hot. Add chicken; cook and stir 7 to 10 minutes or until browned and no longer pink in center. Cool slightly.

2 Combine chicken, tomato, cucumber and onion in medium bowl. Drizzle with vinegar and oil; toss to coat. Sprinkle with oregano, mint and salt; toss to combine.

3 Place 1 lettuce leaf in each pita bread half, if desired. Divide chicken mixture evenly; spoon into pita bread halves.   *Makes 6 servings*

Nutrients per Serving:

Calories	242
(21% of calories from fat)	
Total Fat	6 g
Saturated Fat	1 g
Cholesterol	50 mg
Sodium	353 mg
Carbohydrate	24 g
Dietary Fiber	2 g
Protein	23 g
Calcium	57 mg
Iron	2 mg
Vitamin A	30 RE
Vitamin C	7 mg

DIETARY EXCHANGES:
1½ Starch/Bread, 2½ Lean Meat

TARRAGON CHICKEN SALAD SANDWICHES

❖

Fresh grapes are added to this chicken salad for a burst of flavor and nutritional value. Besides supplying fiber and vitamin A, grapes are low in calories, which makes them a great snack food. Green grapes that have a tinge of yellow and red grapes that are predominantly crimson will be the sweetest.

❖

1¼ pounds boneless skinless chicken breasts, cooked
1 cup thinly sliced celery
1 cup seedless red or green grapes, cut into halves
½ cup raisins
½ cup plain nonfat yogurt
¼ cup reduced fat mayonnaise or salad dressing
2 tablespoons finely chopped shallots or onion
2 tablespoons minced fresh tarragon *or* 1 teaspoon dried tarragon leaves
½ teaspoon salt
⅛ teaspoon white pepper
6 lettuce leaves
6 whole wheat buns, split

1 Cut chicken into scant ½-inch pieces. Combine chicken, celery, grapes and raisins in large bowl. Combine yogurt, mayonnaise, shallots, tarragon, salt and pepper in small bowl. Spoon over chicken mixture; mix lightly.

2 Place 1 lettuce leaf in each bun. Divide chicken mixture evenly; spoon into buns.

Makes 6 servings

Nutrients per Serving:

Calories	353
(18% of calories from fat)	
Total Fat	7 g
Saturated Fat	1 g
Cholesterol	76 mg
Sodium	509 mg
Carbohydrate	41 g
Dietary Fiber	4 g
Protein	34 g
Calcium	120 mg
Iron	2 mg
Vitamin A	62 RE
Vitamin C	6 mg

DIETARY EXCHANGES:
1½ Starch/Bread, 4 Lean Meat, ½ Fruit

❖

Health Tip:
Be sure to read the ingredient list before purchasing whole wheat bread products. The first ingredient listed should be *whole* wheat flour, not wheat flour. Whole wheat flour contains the wheat germ, which increases the fiber and overall nutritional content of the final product.

❖

PITA PIZZAS

❖

Pita, or pocket bread, is a flat bread served throughout the Middle East, either as an accompaniment to meals, stuffed to form sandwiches, or cut into wedges to serve as dippers. Using whole wheat pita breads as the chewy crust for these mini-pizzas provides an extra boost of vitamins, minerals and fiber.

❖

Nonstick cooking spray
½ pound boneless skinless chicken breasts, cut into ½-inch cubes
½ cup thinly sliced red bell pepper
½ cup thinly sliced mushrooms
½ cup thinly sliced red onion (about 1 small)
2 cloves garlic, minced
1 teaspoon dried basil leaves
½ teaspoon dried oregano leaves
1 cup torn fresh spinach leaves
6 mini whole wheat pita breads
½ cup (2 ounces) shredded part-skim mozzarella cheese
1 tablespoon grated Parmesan cheese

1 Preheat oven to 375°F. Spray medium nonstick skillet with cooking spray; heat over medium heat until hot. Add chicken; cook and stir 6 minutes or until browned and no longer pink in center. Remove chicken from skillet.

2 Spray same nonstick skillet again with cooking spray; add bell pepper, mushrooms, onion, garlic, basil and oregano. Cook and stir over medium heat 5 to 7 minutes or until vegetables are crisp-tender. Return chicken to skillet; stir well.

3 Place spinach on top of pita breads. Divide chicken and vegetable mixture evenly; spoon over spinach. Sprinkle evenly with mozzarella and Parmesan cheese. Bake, uncovered, 7 to 10 minutes or until cheese is melted.   *Makes 6 servings*

Nutrients per Serving:

Calories	158
(17% of calories from fat)	
Total Fat	3 g
Saturated Fat	2 g
Cholesterol	125 mg
Sodium	198 mg
Carbohydrate	19 g
Dietary Fiber	4 g
Protein	14 g
Calcium	119 mg
Iron	2 mg
Vitamin A	99 RE
Vitamin C	21 mg

DIETARY EXCHANGES:
1 Starch/Bread, 1½ Lean Meat, ½ Vegetable

CHICKEN AND MOZZARELLA MELTS

Mozzarella is a soft white cheese that melts easily. In southern Italy, where it originated, it is made from the milk of buffaloes. In other parts of Italy and North America, it is made from cow's milk.

❖

Nutrients per Serving:

Calories	299
(16% of calories from fat)	
Total Fat	5 g
Saturated Fat	3 g
Cholesterol	47 mg
Sodium	498 mg
Carbohydrate	37 g
Dietary Fiber	3 g
Protein	27 g
Calcium	188 mg
Iron	3 mg
Vitamin A	198 RE
Vitamin C	24 mg

DIETARY EXCHANGES:
2 Starch/Bread, 2½ Lean
Meat, 1 Vegetable

---

 2 cloves garlic, crushed
 4 boneless skinless chicken breast halves (¾ pound)
   Nonstick cooking spray
 ⅛ teaspoon salt
 ⅛ teaspoon pepper
 1 tablespoon prepared pesto sauce
 4 small hard rolls, split
12 fresh spinach leaves
 8 fresh basil leaves* (optional)
 3 plum tomatoes, sliced
 ½ cup (2 ounces) shredded part-skim mozzarella cheese

1 Preheat oven to 350°F. Rub garlic on all surfaces of chicken. Spray medium nonstick skillet with cooking spray; heat over medium heat until hot. Add chicken; cook 5 to 6 minutes on each side or until no longer pink in center. Sprinkle with salt and pepper.

2 Brush pesto sauce on bottom halves of rolls; layer with spinach, basil, if desired, and tomatoes. Place chicken in rolls; sprinkle cheese evenly over chicken. (If desired, sandwiches may be prepared up to this point and wrapped in aluminum foil. Refrigerate until ready to bake. Bake in preheated 350°F oven until chicken is warm, about 20 minutes.)

3 Wrap sandwiches in aluminum foil; bake about 10 minutes or until cheese is melted.

Makes 4 servings

*Omit basil leaves if fresh are unavailable. Do not substitute dried basil leaves.

MEATBALL GRINDERS

❖

❖

Nutrients per Serving:

Calories	340
(17% of calories from fat)	
Total Fat	7 g
Saturated Fat	2 g
Cholesterol	63 mg
Sodium	702 mg
Carbohydrate	40 g
Dietary Fiber	3 g
Protein	31 g
Calcium	121 mg
Iron	3 mg
Vitamin A	94 RE
Vitamin C	16 mg

DIETARY EXCHANGES:
2 Starch/Bread, 3 Lean Meat, 1½ Vegetable

1 pound ground chicken
½ cup fresh whole wheat or white bread crumbs (1 slice bread)
1 egg white
3 tablespoons finely chopped fresh parsley
2 cloves garlic, minced
¼ teaspoon salt
⅛ teaspoon pepper
  Nonstick cooking spray
¼ cup chopped onion
1 can (8 ounces) whole tomatoes, drained and coarsely chopped
1 can (4 ounces) reduced sodium tomato sauce
1 teaspoon dried Italian seasoning
4 small hard rolls, split
2 tablespoons grated Parmesan cheese

1 Combine chicken, bread crumbs, egg white, parsley, garlic, salt and pepper in medium bowl. Form mixture into 12 to 16 meatballs. Spray medium nonstick skillet with cooking spray; heat over medium heat until hot. Add meatballs; cook and stir about 5 minutes or until browned on all sides. Remove meatballs from skillet.

2 Add onion to skillet; cook and stir 2 to 3 minutes. Stir in tomatoes, tomato sauce and Italian seasoning; heat to a boil. Reduce heat to low and simmer, covered, 15 minutes. Return meatballs to skillet; simmer, covered, 15 minutes.

3 Place 3 to 4 meatballs in each roll. Divide sauce evenly; spoon over meatballs. Sprinkle with cheese.

Makes 4 servings

SALADS

CHICKEN AND COUSCOUS SALAD

A staple of North African cuisine, couscous is a quick-cooking grain with many uses. It can be served with milk as a cereal, in casseroles or stuffings, or tossed with dressing for a salad, as it is here.

Nutrients per Serving:

Calories	348
(20% of calories from fat)	
Total Fat	8 g
Saturated Fat	1 g
Cholesterol	58 mg
Sodium	85 mg
Carbohydrate	43 g
Dietary Fiber	9 g
Protein	27 g
Calcium	59 mg
Iron	2 mg
Vitamin A	143 RE
Vitamin C	150 mg

DIETARY EXCHANGES:
1½ Starch/Bread, 2½ Lean Meat, ½ Fruit, 2½ Vegetable

1 can (14½ ounces) low sodium chicken broth, defatted
½ teaspoon ground cinnamon
¼ teaspoon ground nutmeg
¼ teaspoon curry powder
1 cup uncooked couscous
1½ pounds boneless skinless chicken breasts, cooked
2 cups fresh pineapple chunks
2 cups cubed seeded cucumber chunks
2 cups cubed red bell pepper
2 cups cubed yellow bell pepper
1 cup sliced celery
½ cup sliced green onions with tops
3 tablespoons apple cider vinegar
3 tablespoons water
2 tablespoons vegetable oil
1 tablespoon fresh mint *or* 1 teaspoon dried mint leaves
Lettuce leaves

1 In nonstick Dutch oven or large nonstick saucepan, heat chicken broth, cinnamon, nutmeg and curry powder to a boil. Stir in couscous; remove pan from heat and let stand, covered, 5 minutes. Fluff couscous with fork; cool to room temperature.

2 Cut chicken into ½-inch pieces. Add chicken, pineapple, cucumber, bell peppers, celery and green onions to couscous; toss to combine.

3 In small jar with tight-fitting lid, combine vinegar, water, oil and mint; shake well. Pour over couscous mixture; toss to coat. Serve immediately in lettuce-lined bowl. Garnish as desired.

Makes 6 servings

CHICKEN SALAD NIÇOISE

"Niçoise" refers to the cooking style of Nice, located in southern France. This main-dish salad substitutes chicken for the traditional tuna, but the integral ingredients of tomatoes, beans and potatoes remain.

❖

Nutrients per Serving:

Calories	301
(16% of calories from fat)	
Total Fat	5 g
Saturated Fat	1 g
Cholesterol	40 mg
Sodium	103 mg
Carbohydrate	42 g
Dietary Fiber	3 g
Protein	23 g
Calcium	104 mg
Iron	4 mg
Vitamin A	85 RE
Vitamin C	27 mg

DIETARY EXCHANGES:
2 Starch/Bread, 2 Lean Meat, 1½ Vegetable

Nonstick cooking spray
1 pound chicken tenders
½ cup red onion wedges (about 1 small)
 Fresh spinach leaves (optional)
2 cups whole green beans, cooked and chilled
2 cups cubed red potatoes, cooked and chilled
2 cups halved cherry tomatoes
1 can (15½ ounces) Great Northern beans, drained and rinsed
 Herb and Mustard Dressing (recipe follows)

1 Spray medium nonstick skillet with cooking spray; heat over medium heat until hot. Add chicken; cook and stir 7 to 10 minutes or until chicken is browned and no longer pink in center. Cool slightly; refrigerate until chilled.

2 Spray small nonstick skillet with cooking spray; heat over medium heat until hot. Add onion; cook and stir over low heat about 15 minutes or until onions are caramelized. Cool to room temperature.

3 Place spinach, if desired, on plates. Top with chicken, onions, green beans, potatoes, tomatoes and Great Northern beans. Drizzle with Herb and Mustard Dressing. Serve immediately. *Makes 6 servings*

HERB AND MUSTARD DRESSING

¼ cup water
3 tablespoons balsamic or cider vinegar
1½ tablespoons Dijon-style mustard
1 tablespoon olive oil
1 teaspoon dried basil leaves
1 teaspoon dried thyme leaves
1 teaspoon dried rosemary
1 small clove garlic, minced

1 In small jar with tight-fitting lid, combine all ingredients; shake well. Refrigerate until ready to use; shake before using. *Makes about ⅔ cup*

BLACKENED CHICKEN SALAD

Nutrients per Serving:

*includes Ranch Salad
Dressing*

Calories	249
(25% of calories from fat)	
Total Fat	7 g
Saturated Fat	1 g
Cholesterol	59 mg
Sodium	369 mg
Carbohydrate	21 g
Dietary Fiber	5 g
Protein	27 g
Calcium	137 mg
Iron	5 mg
Vitamin A	664 RE
Vitamin C	45 mg

DIETARY EXCHANGES:
1 Starch/Bread, 2½ Lean
Meat, 1½ Vegetable

2 cups cubed sourdough or French bread
　Nonstick cooking spray
1 tablespoon paprika
1 teaspoon onion powder
1 teaspoon garlic powder
½ teaspoon dried oregano leaves
½ teaspoon dried thyme leaves
½ teaspoon white pepper
½ teaspoon ground red pepper
½ teaspoon black pepper
1 pound boneless skinless chicken breasts
4 cups bite-size pieces fresh spinach leaves
2 cups bite-size pieces romaine lettuce
2 cups cubed zucchini
2 cups cubed seeded cucumber
½ cup sliced green onions with tops
1 medium tomato, cut into 8 wedges
　Ranch Salad Dressing (recipe page 34)

1 Preheat oven to 375°F. To make croutons, spray bread cubes lightly with cooking spray; place in 15 × 10-inch jelly-roll pan. Bake 10 to 15 minutes or until browned, stirring occasionally.

2 Combine paprika, onion powder, garlic powder, oregano, thyme, white pepper, red pepper and black pepper in small bowl; rub on all surfaces of chicken. Broil chicken, 6 inches from heat source, 7 to 8 minutes on each side or until chicken is no longer pink in center. Or, grill chicken, on covered grill over medium-hot coals, 10 minutes on each side or until chicken is no longer pink in center. Cool slightly. Cut chicken into thin strips.

3 Combine warm chicken, greens, zucchini, cucumber, green onions, tomato and croutons in large bowl. Drizzle with Ranch Salad Dressing; toss to coat. Serve immediately.

Makes 4 servings

(continued on page 34)

Blackened Chicken Salad, continued

RANCH SALAD DRESSING

¼ cup water
3 tablespoons reduced calorie cucumber-ranch salad dressing
1 tablespoon reduced fat mayonnaise or salad dressing
1 tablespoon lemon juice
2 teaspoons minced fresh parsley
⅛ teaspoon salt
⅛ teaspoon pepper

1 In small jar with tight-fitting lid, combine all ingredients; shake well. Refrigerate until ready to use; shake before using.   *Makes about ½ cup*

❖
Cook's Tip
Cooking methods often turn low fat food into a high fat dish simply
by using oil for cooking or to prevent sticking to the pan. Naturally low
in fat, skinless chicken breasts remain that way by broiling
or grilling.
❖

CHICKEN, TORTELLINI AND ROASTED VEGETABLE SALAD

❖

Roasting vegetables at high heat gives them a wonderful new flavor complexity without adding any fat. Combine them with low fat tortellini and tender chicken to make this a vitamin-rich salad.

❖

3 cups whole medium mushrooms
2 cups cubed zucchini
2 cups cubed eggplant
¾ cup red onion wedges (about 1 medium)
  Nonstick olive oil cooking spray
1½ packages (9-ounce size) reduced fat cheese tortellini
6 cups bite-size pieces leaf lettuce and arugula
1 pound boneless skinless chicken breasts, cooked and cut into 1½-inch pieces
  Sun-Dried Tomato and Basil Vinaigrette (recipe page 36)

1 Heat oven to 425°F. Place mushrooms, zucchini, eggplant and onion in 15 × 10-inch jelly-roll pan. Spray generously with cooking spray; toss to coat. Bake 20 to 25 minutes or until vegetables are browned. Cool to room temperature.

2 Cook tortellini according to package directions; drain. Cool to room temperature.

3 Combine roasted vegetables, tortellini, lettuce and chicken in large bowl. Drizzle with Sun-Dried Tomato and Basil Vinaigrette; toss to coat. Serve immediately.

Makes 8 servings

Nutrients per Serving:

includes Sun-Dried Tomato and Basil Vinaigrette

Calories	210
(27% of calories from fat)	
Total Fat	7 g
Saturated Fat	1 g
Cholesterol	31 mg
Sodium	219 mg
Carbohydrate	24 g
Dietary Fiber	3 g
Protein	16 g
Calcium	137 mg
Iron	4 mg
Vitamin A	851 RE
Vitamin C	53 mg

DIETARY EXCHANGES:
1 Starch/Bread, 1½ Lean Meat, 1½ Vegetable, ½ Fat

(continued on page 36)

Chicken, Tortellini and Roasted Vegetable Salad, continued

SUN–DRIED TOMATO AND BASIL VINAIGRETTE

4 sun-dried tomato halves, *not* packed in oil
   Hot water
½ cup defatted low sodium chicken broth
2 tablespoons finely chopped fresh basil *or* 2 teaspoons dried basil leaves
2 tablespoons olive oil
2 tablespoons lemon juice
2 tablespoons water
1 clove garlic, minced
¼ teaspoon salt
¼ teaspoon pepper

1 Place sun-dried tomatoes in small bowl. Pour hot water over tomatoes to cover. Let stand 10 to 15 minutes or until tomatoes are soft. Drain well; chop tomatoes.

2 In small jar with tight-fitting lid, combine tomatoes and remaining ingredients; shake well. Refrigerate until ready to use; shake before using.   *Makes about 1 cup*

❖

Cook's Tip

Look for firm eggplant with smooth skin and uniform color. Usually the smaller the eggplant, the sweeter and more tender it is. Store at room temperature for two days or refrigerate in a plastic bag up to four days.

❖

SZECHUAN CHICKEN SALAD

❖

Traditional Chinese seasonings give an exciting new taste to this salad, served over napa cabbage. Eating cabbage and other cruciferous vegetables (broccoli, cauliflower, Brussels sprouts, kale and turnips) several times a week is recommended for cancer prevention.

❖

1 package (5 ounces) Chinese-style rice noodles
  Nonstick cooking spray
1 pound boneless skinless chicken breasts, cut into 2½-inch pieces
3 cups snow peas
2 cups small broccoli flowerettes
2 cups matchstick size carrot strips
2 cups sliced mushrooms
¼ cup plus 2 tablespoons water, divided
1 teaspoon cornstarch
3 tablespoons reduced sodium soy sauce
3 to 4 teaspoons rice wine vinegar
1 tablespoon sesame oil
1 tablespoon Szechuan hot and spicy all-purpose sauce
½ teaspoon five-spice powder
3 cups coarsely chopped napa cabbage

1 Cook noodles according to package directions; cool to room temperature.

2 Spray wok or large nonstick skillet with cooking spray; heat over medium-high heat until hot. Add chicken; stir-fry 5 to 7 minutes or until browned and no longer pink in center. Remove chicken from wok.

3 Add snow peas, broccoli, carrots, mushrooms and 2 tablespoons water to wok; cook, covered, 2 minutes. Uncover; stir-fry about 5 minutes or until vegetables are crisp-tender. Remove vegetables from wok.

4 Combine remaining ¼ cup water and cornstarch in small bowl; stir in soy sauce, vinegar, oil, hot and spicy sauce and five-spice powder. Add to wok; heat to a boil. Cook 1 minute, stirring constantly. Return chicken and vegetables to wok; toss to coat with cornstarch mixture.

5 Divide cabbage among 6 serving plates; arrange noodles over cabbage. Top with warm chicken mixture. Serve immediately.   *Makes 6 servings*

Nutrients per Serving:

Calories	261
(15% of calories from fat)	
Total Fat	4 g
Saturated Fat	1 g
Cholesterol	37 mg
Sodium	377 mg
Carbohydrate	37 g
Dietary Fiber	5 g
Protein	19 g
Calcium	104 mg
Iron	4 mg
Vitamin A	1,098 RE
Vitamin C	67 mg

DIETARY EXCHANGES:
1½ Starch/Bread, 2 Lean Meat, 1½ Vegetable

TAOS CHICKEN SALAD

❖

Jícama, a large root vegetable, is also referred to as the Mexico potato. It has a sweet, nutty flavor and a crisp texture similar to that of water chestnuts. Jícama is a good source of vitamin C and potassium.

❖

Nutrients per Serving:

Calories	258
(19% of calories from fat)	
Total Fat	6 g
Saturated Fat	1 g
Cholesterol	37 mg
Sodium	437 mg
Carbohydrate	36 g
Dietary Fiber	6 g
Protein	18 g
Calcium	143 mg
Iron	4 mg
Vitamin A	281 RE
Vitamin C	100 mg

DIETARY EXCHANGES:
1½ Starch/Bread, 1½ Lean
Meat, ½ Fruit,
1 Vegetable

---

3 flour or corn tortillas, cut into ¼-inch strips
Nonstick cooking spray
1 pound boneless skinless chicken thighs, cut into strips
6 cups bite-size pieces assorted salad greens
2 oranges, peeled and cut into segments
2 cups peeled jícama strips
1 can (15½ ounces) pinto beans, drained and rinsed
1 cup cubed red bell pepper
½ cup sliced celery
½ cup sliced green onions with tops
Lime Vinaigrette (recipe follows)

1 Preheat oven to 350°F. Spray tortilla strips lightly with cooking spray; place in 15 × 10-inch jelly-roll pan. Bake about 10 minutes or until browned, stirring occasionally. Cool to room temperature.

2 Spray medium nonstick skillet with cooking spray; heat over medium heat until hot. Add chicken; cook and stir about 15 minutes or until no longer pink in center. Refrigerate until chilled.

3 Combine greens, oranges, jícama, beans, bell pepper, celery and green onions in large bowl; add chicken. Drizzle with Lime Vinaigrette; toss to coat. Serve immediately; garnish with tortilla strips.   *Makes 6 servings*

LIME VINAIGRETTE

3 tablespoons finely chopped fresh cilantro or parsley
3 tablespoons plain low fat yogurt
3 tablespoons orange juice
2 tablespoons lime juice
2 tablespoons white wine vinegar
2 tablespoons water
1 tablespoon sugar
1 teaspoon chili powder
½ teaspoon onion powder
½ teaspoon ground cumin

1 In small jar with tight-fitting lid, combine all ingredients; shake well. Refrigerate until ready to use; shake before using.   *Makes about ¾ cup*

SOUPS & STEWS

WHITE BEAN CHILI

❖

In addition to being an excellent source of fiber, legumes (beans, lentils and peas) are also beneficial in lowering blood cholesterol and protecting against colon cancer. Rinse and drain canned beans before using to eliminate excess sodium.

❖

Nonstick cooking spray
1 pound ground chicken
3 cups coarsely chopped celery
1½ cups coarsely chopped onions (about 2 medium)
3 cloves garlic, minced
4 teaspoons chili powder
1½ teaspoons ground cumin
¾ teaspoon ground allspice
¾ teaspoon ground cinnamon
½ teaspoon pepper
1 can (16 ounces) whole tomatoes, undrained and coarsely chopped
1 can (15½ ounces) Great Northern beans, drained and rinsed
2 cups defatted low sodium chicken broth

1 Spray large nonstick skillet with cooking spray; heat over medium heat until hot. Add chicken; cook and stir until browned, breaking into pieces with fork. Remove chicken; drain fat from skillet.

2 Add celery, onions and garlic to skillet; cook and stir over medium heat 5 to 7 minutes or until tender. Sprinkle with chili powder, cumin, allspice, cinnamon and pepper; cook and stir 1 minute.

3 Return chicken to skillet. Stir in tomatoes with juice, beans and chicken broth; heat to a boil. Reduce heat to low and simmer, uncovered, 15 minutes. Garnish as desired.

Makes 6 entree servings

Nutrients per Serving:

Calories	232
(22% of calories from fat)	
Total Fat	6 g
Saturated Fat	1 g
Cholesterol	36 mg
Sodium	241 mg
Carbohydrate	26 g
Dietary Fiber	3 g
Protein	20 g
Calcium	117 mg
Iron	3 mg
Vitamin A	128 RE
Vitamin C	21 mg

DIETARY EXCHANGES:
1 Starch/Bread, 2 Lean
Meat, 2 Vegetable

CHICKEN CACCIATORE

Cacciatore is an Italian word that refers to foods prepared "hunter-style" — a naturally healthy way of cooking with mushrooms, onions, tomatoes and various herbs. This classic chicken dish is served over spaghetti, a good source of complex carbohydrates.

Nutrients per Serving:

Calories	472
(30% of calories from fat)	
Total Fat	16 g
Saturated Fat	4 g
Cholesterol	107 mg
Sodium	470 mg
Carbohydrate	42 g
Dietary Fiber	4 g
Protein	40 g
Calcium	68 mg
Iron	4 mg
Vitamin A	153 RE
Vitamin C	69 mg

DIETARY EXCHANGES:
2½ Starch/Bread, 4½ Lean Meat, 1½ Vegetable, ½ Fat

Nonstick cooking spray
4 pounds chicken pieces (breasts, legs, thighs)
2 cups sliced mushrooms
2 cups chopped green bell peppers
¾ cup coarsely chopped onion (about 1 medium)
3 cloves garlic, minced
1 can (16 ounces) whole tomatoes, undrained and coarsely chopped
¾ cup tomato juice
½ cup water
¼ cup tomato paste
1 tablespoon sugar
2 teaspoons dried rosemary
1 teaspoon dried basil leaves
1 teaspoon dried oregano leaves
½ teaspoon salt
¼ teaspoon black pepper
6 cups hot cooked spaghetti

1 Generously spray nonstick Dutch oven or large nonstick skillet with cooking spray; heat over medium heat until hot. Cook chicken 10 to 15 minutes or until browned on all sides. Drain fat from Dutch oven.

2 Add mushrooms, bell peppers, onion and garlic to Dutch oven; cook and stir 3 to 4 minutes.

3 Stir in canned tomatoes with juice, ¾ cup tomato juice, water, tomato paste, sugar, rosemary, basil, oregano, salt and black pepper; heat to a boil. Reduce heat to low and simmer, covered, 45 minutes. Uncover; simmer about 30 minutes or until chicken is no longer pink in center and juices run clear. Serve over spaghetti. Garnish as desired.

Makes 8 entree servings

CHICKEN AND CORN CHOWDER

❖

This hearty chowder is thickened in a healthful way. A portion of the ingredients are processed in a blender until finely chopped, then added to the rest of the chowder. As a result, milk can be used instead of heavy cream to finish the soup, saving over 30 grams of fat per serving.

❖

Nutrients per Serving:

Calories	292
(14% of calories from fat)	
Total Fat	5 g
Saturated Fat	2 g
Cholesterol	65 mg
Sodium	465 mg
Carbohydrate	36 g
Dietary Fiber	4 g
Protein	29 g
Calcium	151 mg
Iron	2 mg
Vitamin A	874 RE
Vitamin C	9 mg

DIETARY EXCHANGES:
1½ Starch/Bread, 2½ Lean Meat, ½ Milk, ½ Vegetable

Nonstick cooking spray
1 pound boneless skinless chicken breasts, cut into ½-inch pieces
3 cups thawed frozen whole kernel corn
¾ cup coarsely chopped onion (about 1 medium)
1 to 2 tablespoons water
1 cup diced carrots
2 tablespoons finely chopped jalapeño pepper
½ teaspoon dried oregano leaves
¼ teaspoon dried thyme leaves
3 cups defatted low sodium chicken broth
1½ cups 2% milk
½ teaspoon salt

1 Spray large nonstick saucepan with cooking spray; heat over medium heat until hot. Add chicken; cook and stir about 10 minutes or until browned and no longer pink in center. Remove chicken from saucepan.

2 Add corn and onion to saucepan; cook and stir about 5 minutes or until onion is tender. Place 1 cup corn mixture in food processor or blender. Process until finely chopped, adding 1 to 2 tablespoons water to liquify mixture; reserve.

3 Add carrots, jalapeño pepper, oregano and thyme to saucepan; cook and stir about 5 minutes or until corn begins to brown. Return chicken to saucepan. Stir in chicken broth, milk, reserved corn mixture and salt; heat to a boil. Reduce heat to low and simmer, covered, 15 to 20 minutes.

Makes 4 entree servings

GREEK-STYLE CHICKEN STEW

❖

This stew is ideal for the health-conscious way we eat today. It boasts plenty of authentic Greek flavor with eggplant, artichokes and oregano, yet it has just over 350 calories per serving.

❖

Nutrients per Serving:

Calories	353
(14% of calories from fat)	
Total Fat	5 g
Saturated Fat	1 g
Cholesterol	117 mg
Sodium	246 mg
Carbohydrate	32 g
Dietary Fiber	7 g
Protein	41 g
Calcium	76 mg
Iron	4 mg
Vitamin A	29 RE
Vitamin C	10 mg

DIETARY EXCHANGES:
1½ Starch/Bread, 3½ Lean Meat, 2 Vegetable

3 pounds skinless chicken breasts
  Flour
  Nonstick cooking spray
2 cups cubed peeled eggplant
2 cups sliced mushrooms
¾ cup coarsely chopped onion (about 1 medium)
2 cloves garlic, minced
1 teaspoon dried oregano leaves
½ teaspoon dried basil leaves
½ teaspoon dried thyme leaves
2 cups defatted low sodium chicken broth
¼ cup dry sherry *or* defatted low sodium chicken broth
¼ teaspoon salt
¼ teaspoon pepper
1 can (14 ounces) artichoke hearts, drained
3 cups hot cooked wide egg noodles

1 Coat chicken very lightly with flour. Generously spray nonstick Dutch oven or large nonstick skillet with cooking spray; heat over medium heat until hot. Cook chicken 10 to 15 minutes or until browned on all sides. Remove chicken; drain fat from Dutch oven.

2 Add eggplant, mushrooms, onion, garlic, oregano, basil and thyme to Dutch oven; cook and stir over medium heat 5 minutes.

3 Return chicken to Dutch oven. Stir in chicken broth, sherry, salt and pepper; heat to a boil. Reduce heat to low and simmer, covered, about 1 hour or until chicken is no longer pink in center and juices run clear, adding artichoke hearts during last 20 minutes of cooking. Serve over noodles. Garnish as desired.

Makes 6 entree servings

MEXICAN TORTILLA SOUP

Fresh cilantro is used extensively in Mexican cooking. Also called fresh coriander or Chinese parsley, this pungent herb is similar in appearance to flat-leaf parsley.

Nutrients per Serving:

Calories	184
(15% of calories from fat)	
Total Fat	3 g
Saturated Fat	1 g
Cholesterol	58 mg
Sodium	132 mg
Carbohydrate	16 g
Dietary Fiber	4 g
Protein	23 g
Calcium	66 mg
Iron	2 mg
Vitamin A	1,595 RE
Vitamin C	41 mg

DIETARY EXCHANGES:
2½ Lean Meat, 2 Vegetable

Nonstick cooking spray
2 pounds boneless skinless chicken breasts, cut into ½-inch strips
4 cups diced carrots
2 cups sliced celery
1 cup chopped green bell pepper
1 cup chopped onion (about 1 large)
4 cloves garlic, minced
1 teaspoon dried oregano leaves
½ teaspoon ground cumin
1 jalapeño pepper, sliced and seeded
8 cups defatted low sodium chicken broth
1 large tomato, seeded and chopped
4 to 5 tablespoons lime juice
2 (6-inch) corn tortillas, cut into ¼-inch strips
Salt (optional)
3 tablespoons finely chopped cilantro

1 Preheat oven to 350°F. Spray large nonstick saucepan with cooking spray; heat over medium heat until hot. Add chicken; cook and stir about 10 minutes or until browned and no longer pink in center. Add carrots, celery, bell pepper, onion, garlic, oregano, cumin and jalapeño pepper; cook and stir over medium heat 5 minutes.

2 Stir in chicken broth, tomato and lime juice; heat to a boil. Reduce heat to low and simmer, covered, 15 to 20 minutes.

3 Meanwhile, spray tortilla strips lightly with cooking spray; sprinkle very lightly with salt, if desired. Place on baking sheet. Bake about 10 minutes or until browned and crisp, stirring occasionally.

4 Stir cilantro into soup. Ladle soup into bowls; top with tortilla strips.

Makes 8 entree servings

CHICKEN FRICASSEE

This main-dish stew combines three favorites— hearty chicken, crunchy carrots and tender pasta. A low fat white sauce made with chicken broth, milk and flour gets a delicious flavor boost from dill.

❖

Nutrients per Serving:

Calories	565
(30% of calories from fat)	
Total Fat	19 g
Saturated Fat	5 g
Cholesterol	158 mg
Sodium	357 mg
Carbohydrate	52 g
Dietary Fiber	6 g
Protein	43 g
Calcium	110 mg
Iron	4 mg
Vitamin A	2,226 RE
Vitamin C	10 mg

DIETARY EXCHANGES:
3 Starch/Bread, 4½ Lean
Meat, 2 Vegetable, 1 Fat

3 pounds chicken pieces (breasts, legs, thighs)
Flour
Nonstick cooking spray
3 cups defatted low sodium chicken broth
1 bay leaf
1 pound whole baby carrots
¾ cup onion wedges (about 1 medium)
1 tablespoon margarine
3 tablespoons flour
¾ cup skim milk
1 tablespoon lemon juice
3 tablespoons minced fresh dill *or* 2 teaspoons dried dill weed
1 teaspoon sugar
½ teaspoon salt
6 cups hot cooked noodles

1 Coat chicken pieces very lightly with flour. Spray large nonstick skillet with cooking spray; heat over medium heat until hot. Cook chicken 10 to 15 minutes or until browned on all sides. Drain fat from skillet.

2 Add chicken broth and bay leaf to skillet; heat to a boil. Reduce heat to low and simmer, covered, about 1 hour or until chicken is no longer pink in center and juices run clear, adding carrots and onion during last 20 minutes of cooking.

3 Transfer chicken and vegetables with slotted spoon to platter; keep warm. Heat broth to a boil; boil until broth is reduced to 1 cup. Discard bay leaf.

4 Melt margarine in small saucepan over low heat; stir in 3 tablespoons flour. Cook and stir 1 to 2 minutes. Stir in broth, milk and lemon juice; heat to a boil. Boil until thickened, stirring constantly. Stir in dill, sugar and salt. Arrange chicken over noodles on serving plates; top with sauce. Garnish as desired.

Makes 6 entree servings

CHICKEN RAVIOLI SOUP

Won ton wrappers are paper-thin sheets of dough cut into squares that are available in the produce section of the supermarket. In this soup recipe, they are stuffed with a seasoned low fat ground chicken mixture for a hurry-up version of ravioli.

Chicken Ravioli (recipe follows)
8 cups defatted low sodium chicken broth
2 cups sliced fresh spinach leaves
1 cup sliced carrots
¼ teaspoon salt
⅛ teaspoon pepper

1 Prepare Chicken Ravioli.

2 In large saucepan, heat chicken broth, spinach, carrots, salt and pepper to a boil. Reduce heat to low and simmer, covered, 10 minutes.

3 Return soup to a boil; add Chicken Ravioli. Reduce heat to low and simmer, uncovered, 2 to 3 minutes or until ravioli are tender and rise to surface of soup.

Makes 6 appetizer servings

CHICKEN RAVIOLI

⅓ cup ground chicken
1 tablespoon minced shallot or onion
1 clove garlic, minced
⅛ teaspoon salt
⅛ teaspoon ground nutmeg
⅛ teaspoon pepper
24 won ton wrappers
Water

1 Combine chicken, shallot, garlic, salt, nutmeg and pepper in small bowl. Place rounded teaspoonful of chicken mixture in center of each of 12 won ton wrappers. Moisten edges of won ton wrappers with water. Top with remaining won ton wrappers; press to seal edges. Refrigerate, covered, until ready to cook. *Makes 12 ravioli*

Nutrients per Serving:

Calories	130
(14% of calories from fat)	
Total Fat	2 g
Saturated Fat	<1 g
Cholesterol	26 mg
Sodium	205 mg
Carbohydrate	21 g
Dietary Fiber	2 g
Protein	7 g
Calcium	45 mg
Iron	2 mg
Vitamin A	667 RE
Vitamin C	7 mg

DIETARY EXCHANGES:
1½ Lean Meat, 1 Vegetable

CHICKEN BOURGUIGNONNE

❖

Wild rice is actually the seed of a marsh grass rather than a type of rice. Its nutty flavor and chewy texture make it a perfect accompaniment to all kinds of poultry. A half cup of cooked wild rice has about ten times the amount of folic acid as white rice.

Folic acid is a nutrient important for the formation and growth of red blood cells.

❖

Nutrients per Serving:

Calories	396
(18% of calories from fat)	
Total Fat	8 g
Saturated Fat	2 g
Cholesterol	92 mg
Sodium	251 mg
Carbohydrate	36 g
Dietary Fiber	4 g
Protein	35 g
Calcium	62 mg
Iron	4 mg
Vitamin A	1,639 RE
Vitamin C	14 mg

DIETARY EXCHANGES:
2 Starch/Bread, 3½ Lean Meat, 2½ Vegetable

4 pounds skinless chicken thighs and breasts
  Flour
  Nonstick cooking spray
2 cups defatted low sodium chicken broth
2 cups dry white wine or defatted low sodium chicken broth
1 pound whole baby carrots
¼ cup tomato paste
4 cloves garlic, minced
½ teaspoon dried thyme leaves
2 bay leaves
¼ teaspoon salt
¼ teaspoon pepper
8 ounces fresh or thawed frozen pearl onions
8 ounces whole medium mushrooms
2 cups hot cooked white rice
2 cups hot cooked wild rice
¼ cup minced fresh parsley

1 Preheat oven to 325°F. Coat chicken very lightly with flour. Generously spray nonstick ovenproof Dutch oven or large nonstick ovenproof skillet with cooking spray; heat over medium heat until hot. Cook chicken 10 to 15 minutes or until browned on all sides. Drain fat from Dutch oven.

2 Add chicken broth, wine, carrots, tomato paste, garlic, thyme, bay leaves, salt and pepper to Dutch oven; heat to a boil. Cover; transfer to oven. Bake 1 hour. Add onions and mushrooms. Uncover; bake about 35 minutes or until vegetables are tender and chicken is no longer pink in center and juices run clear. Remove bay leaves. Combine white and wild rice; serve with chicken. Sprinkle rice with parsley.

Makes 8 servings

ENTREES

CHICKEN CORDON BLEU

Pounding boneless chicken breasts to a uniform thickness flattens them so that a savory ham and cheese filling can be easily rolled up inside.

6 boneless skinless chicken breast halves (1¼ pounds)
1 tablespoon Dijon-style mustard
3 slices (1 ounce each) lean ham, cut into halves
3 slices (1 ounce each) reduced fat Swiss cheese, cut into halves
  Nonstick cooking spray
¼ cup unseasoned dry bread crumbs
2 tablespoons minced fresh parsley
3 cups hot cooked rice

1 Preheat oven to 350°F. Pound chicken breasts between 2 pieces of plastic wrap to ¼-inch thickness using flat side of meat mallet or rolling pin. Brush mustard on 1 side of each chicken breast; layer 1 slice each of ham and cheese over mustard. Roll up each chicken breast from short end; secure with wooden picks. Spray tops of chicken rolls with cooking spray; sprinkle with bread crumbs.

2 Arrange chicken rolls in 11 × 7-inch baking pan. Cover; bake 10 minutes. Uncover; bake about 20 minutes or until chicken is no longer pink in center.

3 Stir parsley into rice; serve with chicken. Serve with vegetables if desired.

Makes 6 servings

Nutrients per Serving:

Calories	297
(18% of calories from fat)	
Total Fat	6 g
Saturated Fat	2 g
Cholesterol	55 mg
Sodium	294 mg
Carbohydrate	32 g
Dietary Fiber	1 g
Protein	27 g
Calcium	166 mg
Iron	2 mg
Vitamin A	46 RE
Vitamin C	5 mg

DIETARY EXCHANGES:
2 Starch/Bread, 2 Lean Meat

Health Note
Boneless skinless chicken breasts are a favorite choice for today's cook because of their quick-cooking appeal and low fat, high protein content.

CHICKEN AND VEGETABLE RISOTTO

❖

Arborio rice, used in this recipe, is a type of short-grain rice grown in Italy; it can be purchased in large supermarkets and Italian groceries. If you prepare the risotto with regular converted rice, you may not need to use all of the broth.

❖

Nonstick olive oil cooking spray
2 cups sliced mushrooms
½ cup chopped onion (about 1 small)
4 cloves garlic, minced
¼ cup finely chopped fresh parsley *or* 1 tablespoon dried parsley leaves
3 to 4 tablespoons finely chopped fresh basil *or* 1 tablespoon dried basil leaves
6 cups defatted low sodium chicken broth
1½ cups uncooked arborio rice *or* converted rice
2 cups broccoli flowerettes, cooked crisp-tender
1 pound chicken tenders, cut into ½-inch pieces and cooked
4 plum tomatoes, seeded and chopped
½ teaspoon salt
½ teaspoon pepper
2 tablespoons grated Parmesan or Romano cheese

1 Spray large nonstick saucepan with cooking spray; heat over medium heat until hot. Add mushrooms, onion and garlic; cook and stir about 5 minutes or until tender. Add parsley and basil; cook and stir 1 minute.

2 Heat chicken broth to a boil in medium saucepan. Reduce heat to low; simmer.

3 Add rice to mushroom mixture; cook and stir over medium heat 1 to 2 minutes. Add chicken broth to mushroom mixture, ½ cup at a time, stirring constantly until broth is absorbed before adding next ½ cup. Continue adding broth and stirring until rice is tender and mixture is creamy, 20 to 25 minutes.

4 Add broccoli, chicken, tomatoes, salt and pepper. Cook and stir 2 to 3 minutes or until heated through. Sprinkle with cheese.

Makes 4 servings

Nutrients per Serving:

Calories	457
(9% of calories from fat)	
Total Fat	5 g
Saturated Fat	1 g
Cholesterol	48 mg
Sodium	449 mg
Carbohydrate	74 g
Dietary Fiber	5 g
Protein	29 g
Calcium	153 mg
Iron	7 mg
Vitamin A	225 RE
Vitamin C	90 mg

DIETARY EXCHANGES:
4 Starch/Bread, 2 Lean Meat, 2½ Vegetable

GRILLED CHICKEN WITH SOUTHERN BARBECUE SAUCE

❖

Grilling—and its indoor counterpart, broiling—is a very healthy cooking method since it allows fat to drip away from food during cooking. In any recipe calling for chicken pieces, always use tongs to turn chicken pieces while cooking. This prevents the meat from being pierced, keeping the natural juices sealed inside.

❖

Nonstick cooking spray
½ cup chopped onion (about 1 small)
4 cloves garlic, minced
1 can (16 ounces) no-salt-added tomato sauce
¾ cup water
3 tablespoons firmly packed light brown sugar
3 tablespoons chili sauce
2 teaspoons chili powder
2 teaspoons dried thyme leaves
2 teaspoons white Worcestershire sauce
¾ teaspoon ground red pepper
½ teaspoon ground cinnamon
½ teaspoon black pepper
6 skinless chicken breast halves (2¼ pounds)
6 medium Idaho potatoes, baked, hot

1 Spray medium nonstick skillet with cooking spray; heat over medium heat until hot. Add onion and garlic; cook and stir about 5 minutes or until tender. Stir in tomato sauce, water, sugar, chili sauce, chili powder, thyme, Worcestershire sauce, red pepper, cinnamon and black pepper; heat to a boil. Reduce heat to low and simmer, uncovered, 30 minutes or until mixture is reduced to 1½ cups. Pour ¾ cup sauce into small bowl for basting; reserve.

2 Grill chicken, on covered grill over medium-hot coals, 40 to 45 minutes or until chicken is no longer pink in center and juices run clear, turning chicken several times and basting occasionally with reserved sauce.

3 Heat remaining sauce in skillet over medium heat until hot; spoon over chicken. Serve with potatoes. Serve with additional vegetables, if desired.

Makes 6 servings

Nutrients per Serving:

Calories	357
(8% of calories from fat)	
Total Fat	3 g
Saturated Fat	1 g
Cholesterol	69 mg
Sodium	218 mg
Carbohydrate	51 g
Dietary Fiber	5 g
Protein	30 g
Calcium	61 mg
Iron	3 mg
Vitamin A	132 RE
Vitamin C	11 mg

DIETARY EXCHANGES:
2 Starch/Bread, 3 Lean Meat, 2 Vegetable

RICOTTA STUFFED CHICKEN WITH SUN-DRIED TOMATO LINGUINE

❖

Sun-dried tomatoes are a new addition to many supermarket produce departments. These chewy tomatoes have a sweet taste and add a rich tomato flavor to soups, stews and sauces.

❖

Nutrients per Serving:

includes Sun-Dried Tomato Linguine

Calories	529
(26% of calories from fat)	
Total Fat	15 g
Saturated Fat	4 g
Cholesterol	135 mg
Sodium	232 mg
Carbohydrate	54 g
Dietary Fiber	4 g
Protein	45 g
Calcium	150 mg
Iron	5 mg
Vitamin A	1,590 RE
Vitamin C	35 mg

DIETARY EXCHANGES:
3 Starch/Bread, 4½ Lean Meat, 2 Vegetable, ½ Fat

---

1 broiler-fryer chicken (3 pounds)
1 cup reduced fat ricotta cheese
1 cup chopped fresh spinach leaves
4 cloves garlic, minced
2 teaspoons dried basil leaves
2 teaspoons minced fresh parsley
1 teaspoon dried oregano leaves
¼ teaspoon salt
  Nonstick olive oil cooking spray
  Paprika
  Sun-Dried Tomato Linguine (recipe page 66)

1 Preheat oven to 375°F. Split chicken in half with sharp knife or poultry shears, cutting through breastbone. Place chicken, skin side up, on counter and press with palm of hand to crack bone so that chicken will lie flat.

2 Loosen skin over top of chicken using fingers and sharp paring knife; do not loosen skin over wings and drumsticks.

3 Combine ricotta cheese, spinach, garlic, basil, parsley, oregano and salt in small bowl. Stuff mixture under skin of chicken, using small rubber spatula or spoon.

4 Place chicken in roasting pan. Spray top of chicken lightly with cooking spray; sprinkle with paprika. Bake about 1 hour 15 minutes or until chicken is no longer pink in center and juices run clear. Serve with Sun-Dried Tomato Linguine. Garnish as desired.

Makes 6 servings

(continued on page 66)

Ricotta Stuffed Chicken With Sun-Dried Tomato Linguine, continued

SUN–DRIED TOMATO LINGUINE

6 sun-dried tomato halves, *not* packed in oil
  Hot water
  Nonstick olive oil cooking spray
1 cup sliced mushrooms
3 cloves garlic, minced
1 tablespoon minced fresh parsley
¾ teaspoon dried rosemary
1 can (15 ounces) low sodium chicken broth, defatted
2 tablespoons cornstarch
¼ cup cold water
1 package (9 ounces) linguine, cooked in salted water, drained, hot

1 Place sun-dried tomatoes in small bowl; pour hot water over to cover. Let stand 10 to 15 minutes or until tomatoes are soft. Drain well; cut tomatoes into quarters.

2 Spray medium nonstick skillet with cooking spray; heat over medium heat until hot. Add mushrooms and garlic; cook and stir about 5 minutes or until tender. Add sun-dried tomatoes, parsley and rosemary; cook and stir 1 minute.

3 Stir chicken broth into vegetable mixture; heat to a boil. Combine cornstarch and cold water in small bowl; stir into chicken broth mixture. Boil 1 to 2 minutes, stirring constantly. Pour mixture over linguine; toss to coat. *Makes 6 servings*

CHICKEN AND VEGGIE LASAGNA

Pasta is a great source of complex carbohydrates. It also contains six essential amino acids, three B-complex vitamins and iron. When cooking pasta, make sure the water is at a rolling boil. This circulates the pasta so that it cooks evenly.

Nutrients per Serving:

includes Tomato-Herb Sauce

Calories	254
(27% of calories from fat)	
Total Fat	8 g
Saturated Fat	2 g
Cholesterol	51 mg
Sodium	431 mg
Carbohydrate	26 g
Dietary Fiber	4 g
Protein	22 g
Calcium	154 mg
Iron	3 mg
Vitamin A	480 RE
Vitamin C	29 mg

DIETARY EXCHANGES:
1 Starch/Bread, 2 Lean Meat, 2 Vegetable, ½ Fruit

Tomato-Herb Sauce (recipe page 68)
Nonstick olive oil cooking spray
1½ cups thinly sliced zucchini
1 cup thinly sliced carrots
3 cups torn fresh spinach leaves
½ teaspoon salt
1 package (15 ounces) fat free ricotta cheese
½ cup grated Parmesan cheese
9 lasagna noodles, cooked and drained
2 cups (8 ounces) reduced fat shredded mozzarella cheese

1 Prepare Tomato-Herb Sauce.

2 Preheat oven to 350°F. Spray large nonstick skillet with cooking spray; heat over medium heat until hot. Add zucchini and carrots; cook and stir about 5 minutes or until almost tender. Remove from heat; stir in spinach and salt.

3 Combine ricotta and Parmesan cheese in small bowl. Spread 1⅔ cups Tomato-Herb Sauce on bottom of 13 × 9-inch baking pan. Top with 3 noodles. Spoon half the ricotta cheese mixture over noodles; spread lightly with spatula. Spoon half the zucchini mixture over ricotta cheese mixture; sprinkle with 1 cup mozzarella cheese. Repeat layers; place remaining 3 noodles on top.

4 Spread remaining Tomato-Herb Sauce over noodles. Cover with aluminum foil; bake 1 hour or until sauce is bubbly. Let stand 5 to 10 minutes; cut into rectangles. Garnish as desired.

Makes 12 servings

(continued on page 68)

Chicken and Veggie Lasagna, continued

TOMATO–HERB SAUCE

    Nonstick olive oil cooking spray
1½ cups chopped onions (about 2 medium)
 4 cloves garlic, minced
 1 tablespoon dried basil leaves
 1 teaspoon dried oregano leaves
 ½ teaspoon dried tarragon leaves
 ¼ teaspoon dried thyme leaves
2½ pounds ripe tomatoes, peeled and cut into wedges
 1 pound ground chicken, cooked, crumbled, drained
 ¾ cup water
 ¼ cup no-salt-added tomato paste
 ½ teaspoon salt
 ½ teaspoon pepper

1 Spray large nonstick skillet with cooking spray; heat over medium heat until hot. Add onions, garlic, basil, oregano, tarragon and thyme; cook and stir about 5 minutes or until onions are tender.

2 Add tomatoes, chicken, water and tomato paste; heat to a boil. Reduce heat to low and simmer, uncovered, about 20 minutes or until sauce is reduced to 5 cups. Stir in salt and pepper. *Makes 5 cups*

Health Note

Recent studies have shown that eating generous amounts of garlic may play a role in protection against heart disease. Results indicate that garlic may cause serum cholesterol levels to drop, help prevent blood clots that lead to heart attacks and strokes and aid in lowering blood pressure.

TEX-MEX CHICKEN

❖

Boneless skinless chicken breasts are a favorite choice for today's cook because of their quick-cooking appeal and their low fat, high protein content. If you skin and debone your own chicken breasts, save the bones and skin in a plastic bag in your freezer to make flavorful homemade chicken stock.

❖

1 teaspoon ground red pepper
¾ teaspoon onion powder
¾ teaspoon garlic powder
½ teaspoon dried basil leaves
½ teaspoon salt, divided
⅛ teaspoon dried oregano leaves
⅛ teaspoon dried thyme leaves
⅛ teaspoon gumbo filé powder*
6 boneless skinless chicken breast halves (1½ pounds)
¾ pound potatoes, cut into 1-inch wedges
  Nonstick cooking spray
¼ teaspoon black pepper

1 Combine ground red pepper, onion powder, garlic powder, basil, ¼ teaspoon salt, oregano, thyme and gumbo filé powder in small bowl. Rub mixture on all surfaces of chicken. Place chicken in single layer in 13 × 9-inch baking pan. Refrigerate, covered, 4 to 8 hours.

2 Preheat oven to 350°F. Place potatoes in medium bowl. Spray potatoes lightly with cooking spray; toss to coat. Sprinkle with remaining ¼ teaspoon salt and black pepper; toss to combine. Add to chicken in pan.

3 Bake, uncovered, 40 to 45 minutes or until potatoes are tender and chicken is no longer pink in center. Or, grill chicken and potatoes, in aluminum foil pan, on covered grill over medium-hot coals, 20 to 30 minutes or until potatoes are tender and chicken is no longer pink in center. Serve with additional vegetables, if desired.

Makes 6 servings

*Gumbo filé powder is a seasoning widely used in Creole cooking. It is available in the spice or gourmet section of most large supermarkets.

Nutrients per Serving:

Calories	262
(9% of calories from fat)	
Total Fat	3 g
Saturated Fat	1 g
Cholesterol	55 mg
Sodium	237 mg
Carbohydrate	36 g
Dietary Fiber	0 g
Protein	24 g
Calcium	25 mg
Iron	2 mg
Vitamin A	18 RE
Vitamin C	23 mg

DIETARY EXCHANGES:
1 Starch/Bread, 2 Lean Meat

CHICKEN FAJITAS

❖

The name of this popular Southwestern dish actually refers to the strips of marinated and grilled skirt steak that are wrapped inside the warmed tortillas. This chicken version eliminates over 80 calories and 10 grams of fat per serving. The vitamin C content soars thanks to lots of crisp-tender bell peppers.

❖

Nutrients per Serving:

Calories	382
(17% of calories from fat)	
Total Fat	7 g
Saturated Fat	2 g
Cholesterol	60 mg
Sodium	421 mg
Carbohydrate	51 g
Dietary Fiber	5 g
Protein	29 g
Calcium	134 mg
Iron	4 mg
Vitamin A	119 RE
Vitamin C	159 mg

DIETARY EXCHANGES:
2 Starch/Bread, 3 Lean Meat, 3 Vegetable

1 pound chicken tenders
¼ cup lime juice
4 cloves garlic, minced, divided
   Nonstick cooking spray
1 cup sliced red bell peppers
1 cup sliced green bell peppers
1 cup sliced yellow bell peppers
¾ cup onion slices (about 1 medium)
½ teaspoon ground cumin
¼ teaspoon salt
¼ teaspoon ground red pepper
8 teaspoons low fat sour cream
8 (6-inch) flour tortillas, warm
   Green onion tops (optional)
   Salsa (optional)

1 Arrange chicken in 11 × 7-inch glass baking dish; add lime juice and 2 cloves minced garlic. Toss to coat. Cover; marinate in refrigerator 30 minutes, stirring occasionally.

2 Spray large nonstick skillet with cooking spray; heat over medium heat until hot. Add chicken mixture; cook and stir 5 to 7 minutes or until chicken is browned and no longer pink in center. Remove from skillet. Drain excess liquid from skillet, if necessary.

3 Add bell peppers, onion and remaining 2 cloves minced garlic to skillet; cook and stir about 5 minutes or until tender. Sprinkle with cumin, salt and ground red pepper. Return chicken to skillet. Cook and stir 1 to 2 minutes.

4 Spread 1 teaspoon sour cream on 1 side of each tortilla. Spoon chicken and pepper mixture over sour cream; roll up tortillas. Tie each tortilla with green onion top, if desired. Serve with salsa, if desired.

Makes 4 servings

CHICKEN POT PIE

Tissue-thin layers of flaky phyllo dough top this pot pie replacing the usual high fat pastry crust. Phyllo dough has typically been used to make classic Greek dishes such as spanakopita and baklava, but because frozen phyllo dough is readily available in supermarkets, its use is becoming more widespread.

❖

Nutrients per Serving:

Calories	266
(17% of calories from fat)	
Total Fat	5 g
Saturated Fat	2 g
Cholesterol	59 mg
Sodium	300 mg
Carbohydrate	32 g
Dietary Fiber	5 g
Protein	23 g
Calcium	50 mg
Iron	2 mg
Vitamin A	1,061 RE
Vitamin C	19 mg

DIETARY EXCHANGES:
1½ Starch/Bread, 2½ Lean Meat, 1 Vegetable

Nonstick cooking spray
¾ pound boneless skinless chicken thighs, cut into 1-inch pieces
¾ pound boneless skinless chicken breasts, cut into 1-inch pieces
2 cups sliced carrots
1½ cups cubed potatoes
1 cup cubed turnip
1 cup fresh peas or thawed frozen peas
½ cup chopped onion (about 1 small)
3 cloves garlic, sliced
1 teaspoon dried basil leaves
½ teaspoon dried marjoram leaves
½ teaspoon dried oregano leaves
½ teaspoon dried tarragon leaves
¼ teaspoon salt
¼ teaspoon pepper
1 cup defatted low sodium chicken broth
3 tablespoons all-purpose flour
⅓ cup cold water
3 sheets thawed frozen phyllo pastry

1 Preheat oven to 425°F. Spray large nonstick skillet with cooking spray; heat over medium heat until hot. Add chicken; cook and stir about 10 minutes or until no longer pink in center. Remove chicken from skillet.

2 Add carrots, potatoes, turnip, peas, onion and garlic to skillet; cook and stir 5 minutes. Sprinkle with basil, marjoram, oregano, tarragon, salt and pepper; cook and stir 1 to 2 minutes. Stir in chicken broth; heat to a boil. Reduce heat to low and simmer, covered, about 10 minutes or until vegetables are tender.

3 Return chicken to skillet; return mixture to a boil. Combine flour and water in small bowl; stir into chicken mixture. Boil 1 minute, stirring constantly. Pour mixture into 1-quart casserole or 10-inch pie plate.

4 Spray 1 sheet phyllo with cooking spray; top with remaining 2 sheets phyllo, spraying each lightly. Place stack of phyllo on top of casserole; cut edges 1 inch larger than casserole. Fold under edges of phyllo. Bake about 15 minutes or until phyllo is brown and crisp.

Makes 6 servings

CHICKEN AND CURRIED FRUIT

❖

The intense, sweet flavor and chewy texture of dried fruit is highlighted by curry and other flavorings in this simple entree. Leftover dried fruit may be sprinkled over cereal or tossed in pilafs or stuffings. Remember that a little goes a long way — although low in fat, dried fruit is higher in calories than fresh fruit.

❖

6 skinless chicken breast halves (2¼ pounds)
1 cup mixed diced dried fruit
½ cup chopped onion (about 1 small)
¼ cup chopped chutney
3 cloves garlic, minced
1 to 1½ teaspoons curry powder
1 teaspoon ground cumin
¼ teaspoon ground red pepper
¼ teaspoon ground allspice
2½ cups defatted low sodium chicken broth
½ cup dry sherry or apple juice
3 cups hot cooked rice or couscous

1 Preheat oven to 350°F. Arrange chicken, breast side up, in single layer in 13 × 9-inch baking pan. Place dried fruit around chicken. Combine onion, chutney, garlic, curry powder, cumin, red pepper and allspice in medium bowl; stir in chicken broth and sherry. Pour mixture over chicken and fruit.

2 Cover; bake 30 minutes. Uncover; bake about 15 minutes or until chicken is no longer pink in center and juices run clear.

3 Remove chicken from pan; arrange over rice on serving platter. Process half the fruit and half the liquid mixture from pan in food processor or blender until smooth; spoon over chicken. Discard remaining liquid mixture. Arrange remaining fruit over chicken.

Makes 6 servings

Nutrients per Serving:

Calories	383
(7% of calories from fat)	
Total Fat	4 g
Saturated Fat	1 g
Cholesterol	69 mg
Sodium	81 mg
Carbohydrate	52 g
Dietary Fiber	3 g
Protein	29 g
Calcium	51 mg
Iron	3 mg
Vitamin A	70 RE
Vitamin C	11 mg

DIETARY EXCHANGES:
2 Starch/Bread, 3 Lean Meat, 1½ Fruit, ½ Vegetable

❖

Cook's Note
Fresh chicken is highly perishable. It can be stored in the coldest part of your refrigerator for two to three days. Once cooked, it will keep for three to four days.

❖

CHEESE RAVIOLI WITH SPINACH PESTO AND CHICKEN

❖

Pesto is a wonderful, fresh-tasting sauce that originated in Italy and is traditionally made with fresh basil leaves. Spinach is substituted in this recipe, providing a powerful punch of iron and vitamins A and C. One pound of raw spinach will yield four cups of leaves.

❖

Cheese Ravioli (recipe page 80) *or* 2 (9-ounce) packages refrigerated low fat ravioli
Spinach Pesto (recipe page 80)
Nonstick cooking spray
¾ cup matchstick size carrot strips
¾ cup thinly sliced celery
½ cup chopped onion (about 1 small)
2 cloves garlic, minced
1 can (14½ ounces) no-salt-added stewed tomatoes
1½ pounds chicken tenders, cut crosswise into halves
¼ cup dry white wine
2 teaspoons dried rosemary
¼ teaspoon salt
⅛ teaspoon pepper

1 Prepare Cheese Ravioli and Spinach Pesto.

2 Spray large nonstick skillet with cooking spray; heat over medium heat until hot. Add carrots, celery, onion and garlic; cook and stir about 5 minutes or until crisp-tender.

3 Add tomatoes, chicken, wine, rosemary, salt and pepper; heat to a boil. Reduce heat to low and simmer, uncovered, about 10 minutes or until vegetables are tender and chicken is no longer pink in center.

4 Arrange Cheese Ravioli on serving plates; spoon chicken and vegetable mixture over ravioli. Top with Spinach Pesto or serve alongside.   *Makes 8 servings*

Nutrients per Serving:

includes Cheese Ravioli and Spinach Pesto

Calories	284
(26% of calories from fat)	
Total Fat	8 g
Saturated Fat	1 g
Cholesterol	74 mg
Sodium	173 mg
Carbohydrate	28 g
Dietary Fiber	3 g
Protein	23 g
Calcium	101 mg
Iron	3 mg
Vitamin A	356 RE
Vitamin C	21 mg

DIETARY EXCHANGES:
1½ Starch/Bread, 2½ Lean Meat, 1½ Vegetable

(continued on page 80)

Cheese Ravioli with Spinach Pesto and Chicken, continued

CHEESE RAVIOLI

Nonstick cooking spray
¼ cup finely chopped onion
2 cloves garlic, minced
2 tablespoons minced fresh parsley
½ teaspoon dried basil leaves
¼ teaspoon *each* dried oregano and dried thyme leaves
⅛ teaspoon pepper
½ cup reduced fat ricotta cheese
32 won ton wrappers
1½ quarts plus 2 tablespoons water, divided
2 teaspoons cornstarch

1 Spray small nonstick skillet with cooking spray; heat over medium heat until hot. Add onion and garlic; cook and stir 2 to 3 minutes or until tender. Sprinkle with parsley, basil, oregano, thyme and pepper; cook and stir 1 minute. Remove from heat; stir in ricotta cheese.

2 Place 2 teaspoons cheese mixture in center of each of 16 won ton wrappers. Combine 2 tablespoons water and cornstarch in small bowl; brush on edges of wrappers. Top with remaining won ton wrappers; press to seal edges.

3 Place remaining 1½ quarts water in large saucepan. Bring to a boil over medium-high heat. Boil 4 to 6 ravioli at a time, uncovered, 2 to 3 minutes or until ravioli are tender and rise to surface of water. Repeat with remaining ravioli.

Makes 8 servings (2 ravioli per serving)

SPINACH PESTO

2 cups loosely packed fresh spinach leaves
2 tablespoons grated Romano cheese
2 tablespoons olive oil or vegetable oil
1 to 2 tablespoons lemon juice
1 tablespoon dried basil leaves
3 cloves garlic, minced

1 Process all ingredients in food processor or blender until smooth.

Makes about 1 cup

TUSCAN CHICKEN BREASTS WITH POLENTA

❖

Cornmeal is ground from dried white or yellow corn and is a versatile grain high in fiber and many essential nutrients. Polenta, a staple of northern Italy, is a mush made from cornmeal. Here, it is cooled until firm, then sliced, lightly browned and topped with an herbed tomato sauce.

❖

Nutrients per Serving:

includes Tuscan Tomato Sauce

Calories	240
(16% of calories from fat)	
Total Fat	4 g
Saturated Fat	1 g
Cholesterol	69 mg
Sodium	345 mg
Carbohydrate	22 g
Dietary Fiber	5 g
Protein	29 g
Calcium	51 mg
Iron	3 mg
Vitamin A	126 RE
Vitamin C	27 mg

DIETARY EXCHANGES:
1 Starch/Bread, 2½ Lean Meat, 1½ Vegetable

4 cups defatted low sodium chicken broth
1 cup yellow cornmeal
½ teaspoon garlic powder
½ teaspoon dried Italian seasoning
¼ teaspoon salt
¼ teaspoon pepper
8 skinless chicken breast halves (3 pounds)
  Nonstick cooking spray
  Fresh spinach leaves, steamed (optional)
  Tuscan Tomato Sauce (recipe page 82)

1 In large nonstick saucepan, heat chicken broth to a boil; slowly stir in cornmeal. Reduce heat to low; cook, stirring frequently, 15 to 20 minutes or until mixture is very thick and pulls away from side of pan. (Mixture may be lumpy.) Pour polenta into greased 9 × 5-inch loaf pan. Cool; refrigerate 2 to 3 hours or until firm.

2 Heat oven to 350°F. Combine garlic powder, Italian seasoning, salt and pepper in small bowl; rub on all surfaces of chicken. Arrange chicken, breast side up, in single layer in 13 × 9-inch baking pan. Bake, uncovered, about 45 minutes or until chicken is no longer pink in center and juices run clear.

3 Remove polenta from pan; transfer to cutting board. Cut polenta crosswise into 16 slices. Cut slices into triangles, if desired. Spray large nonstick skillet with cooking spray; heat over medium heat until hot. Cook polenta about 4 minutes per side or until lightly browned.

4 Place spinach leaves, if desired, on serving plates. Arrange polenta slices and chicken over spinach; top with Tuscan Tomato Sauce. *Makes 8 servings*

(continued on page 82)

Tuscan Chicken Breasts with Polenta, continued

TUSCAN TOMATO SAUCE

Nonstick cooking spray
½ cup chopped onion
2 cloves garlic, minced
8 plum tomatoes, coarsely chopped
1 can (8 ounces) tomato sauce
2 teaspoons dried basil leaves
2 teaspoons dried oregano leaves
2 teaspoons dried rosemary
½ teaspoon pepper

1 Spray medium nonstick saucepan with cooking spray; heat over medium heat until hot. Add onion and garlic; cook and stir about 5 minutes or until tender.

2 Stir in tomatoes, tomato sauce, basil, oregano, rosemary and pepper; heat to a boil. Reduce heat to low and simmer, uncovered, about 6 minutes or until desired consistency, stirring occasionally.

Makes about 3 cups

❖

Cook's Tip

To easily peel garlic, place a clove on a cutting board. Cover the clove with the flat side of a chef's knife blade, then firmly press down on the blade with your fist. This loosens the skin so that it comes right off.

❖

MEDITERRANEAN CHICKEN KABOBS

Nutrients per Serving:

2 kabobs per serving

Calories	293
(23% of calories from fat)	
Total Fat	8 g
Saturated Fat	1 g
Cholesterol	46 mg
Sodium	60 mg
Carbohydrate	34 g
Dietary Fiber	7 g
Protein	22 g
Calcium	56 mg
Iron	3 mg
Vitamin A	49 RE

DIETARY EXCHANGES:
1½ Starch/Bread, 2 Lean Meat, 2 Vegetable, 1½ Fat

2 pounds boneless skinless chicken breasts or chicken tenders, cut into 1-inch pieces
1 small eggplant, cut into 1-inch pieces and peeled
1 medium zucchini, cut crosswise into ½-inch slices
2 medium onions, each cut into 8 wedges
16 medium mushrooms, stems removed
16 cherry tomatoes
1 cup defatted low sodium chicken broth
⅔ cup balsamic vinegar
3 tablespoons olive oil or vegetable oil
2 tablespoons dried mint leaves
4 teaspoons dried basil leaves
1 tablespoon dried oregano leaves
2 teaspoons grated lemon peel
  Chopped fresh parsley (optional)
4 cups hot cooked couscous

1 Alternately thread chicken, eggplant, zucchini, onions, mushrooms and tomatoes onto 16 metal skewers; place in large glass baking dish.

2 Combine chicken broth, vinegar, oil, mint, basil and oregano in small bowl; pour over kabobs. Cover; marinate in refrigerator 2 hours, turning kabobs occasionally.

3 Broil kabobs, 6 inches from heat source, 10 to 15 minutes or until chicken is no longer pink in center, turning kabobs halfway through cooking time. Or, grill kabobs, on covered grill over medium-hot coals, 10 to 15 minutes or until chicken is no longer pink in center, turning kabobs halfway through cooking time. Stir lemon peel and parsley into couscous; serve with kabobs.

Makes 8 servings

CRISPY BAKED CHICKEN

 4 skinless chicken breast halves (1½ pounds)
2½ tablespoons Dijon-style mustard, divided
 1 cup fresh whole wheat bread crumbs (2 slices bread)
 ½ teaspoon dried marjoram leaves
 ½ teaspoon dried thyme leaves
 ¼ teaspoon salt
 ¼ teaspoon dried sage leaves
 ¼ teaspoon black pepper
    Nonstick cooking spray
 1 small red bell pepper, sliced
 2 cloves garlic, minced
 2 cups broccoli flowerettes, cooked crisp-tender
 1 to 2 tablespoons lemon juice

1 Preheat oven to 375°F. Brush tops of chicken breasts with 2 tablespoons mustard. Combine bread crumbs, remaining ½ tablespoon mustard, marjoram, thyme, salt, sage and black pepper in small bowl. Pat mixture evenly over mustard. Arrange chicken, breast side up, in single layer in 13 × 9-inch baking pan.

2 Bake, uncovered, about 40 minutes or until chicken is no longer pink in center and juices run clear.

3 Spray medium nonstick skillet with cooking spray; heat over medium heat until hot. Add bell pepper and garlic; cook and stir about 5 minutes or until tender. Add broccoli and lemon juice; cook and stir 2 to 3 minutes or until heated through.

4 Arrange chicken and broccoli mixture on serving plates.   *Makes 4 servings*

Nutrients per Serving:	
Calories	196
(18% of calories from fat)	
Total Fat	4 g
Saturated Fat	1 g
Cholesterol	69 mg
Sodium	412 mg
Carbohydrate	11 g
Dietary Fiber	3 g
Protein	29 g
Calcium	66 mg
Iron	2 mg
Vitamin A	86 RE
Vitamin C	62 mg

DIETARY EXCHANGES:
½ Starch/Bread, 2½ Lean Meat, 1 Vegetable

❖

Cook's Tip

Mustard is one of the most frequently eaten condiments in the world. One variety, Dijon mustard, is smooth with a slightly hot undertone and is made in Dijon, France. Dijon-style mustard is its American counterpart.

❖

SESAME CHICKEN AND VEGETABLE STIR-FRY

❖

Start on your way toward eating five servings of fruits and vegetables a day with this delicious stir-fry, flavored with traditional Chinese spices and a touch of sesame oil. The combination of broccoli and red peppers contributes over 100% of the daily requirement of vitamin C.

❖

1 tablespoon Oriental sesame oil
1 pound chicken tenders, cut into 1-inch pieces
2 cups broccoli flowerettes
1 small red bell pepper, sliced
½ cup onion slices (about 1 small)
½ cup snow peas
1 can (8 ounces) water chestnuts, sliced and drained
2 cloves garlic, minced
1 teaspoon five-spice powder
1 cup defatted low sodium chicken broth
2 teaspoons cornstarch
2 tablespoons cold water
2 cups hot cooked rice

1 Heat sesame oil in wok or large nonstick skillet over medium heat until hot. Add chicken; stir-fry about 8 minutes or until chicken is no longer pink in center. Remove chicken from wok.

2 Add broccoli, bell pepper, onion, peas, water chestnuts and garlic to wok; stir-fry 5 to 8 minutes or until vegetables are crisp-tender. Sprinkle with five-spice powder; cook and stir 1 minute.

3 Return chicken to wok. Add chicken broth; heat to a boil. Combine cornstarch and water in small bowl; stir into broth mixture. Boil 1 to 2 minutes, stirring constantly. Serve over rice.

Makes 4 servings

Nutrients per Serving:

Calories	354
(19% of calories from fat)	
Total Fat	7 g
Saturated Fat	1 g
Cholesterol	59 mg
Sodium	83 mg
Carbohydrate	44 g
Dietary Fiber	3 g
Protein	27 g
Calcium	64 mg
Iron	3 mg
Vitamin A	89 RE
Vitamin C	71 mg

DIETARY EXCHANGES:
2 Starch/Bread, 3 Lean Meat, 2 Vegetable

❖

Cook's Tip

Oriental sesame oil is an amber-colored oil pressed from toasted sesame seeds. It has a strong, nut-like flavor and is used to accent many Oriental dishes. Sesame oil is high in polyunsaturated fats, which may help to lower blood cholesterol levels.

❖

CHICKEN BAKED IN PARCHMENT

❖

*Baking in parchment paper
seals in natural juices and
flavorings and also
eliminates the need to add
fat. As the food cooks and lets
off steam, the parchment
puffs up into a dome shape.
For a dramatic presentation
at the table, carefully slit the
paper and peel it back to
reveal the food inside.*

❖

Nutrients per Serving:

Calories	321
(9% of calories from fat)	
Total Fat	3 g
Saturated Fat	1 g
Cholesterol	58 mg
Sodium	214 mg
Carbohydrate	41 g
Dietary Fiber	3 g
Protein	28 g
Calcium	45 mg
Iron	2 mg
Vitamin A	810 RE
Vitamin C	42 mg

DIETARY EXCHANGES:
2 Starch/Bread, 2½ Lean
Meat, 1½ Vegetable

Parchment paper
4 boneless skinless chicken breast halves (4 ounces each)
1 cup matchstick size carrot strips
1 cup matchstick size zucchini strips
½ cup snow peas
½ cup thinly sliced red bell pepper
2¼ cups defatted low sodium chicken broth, divided
2 tablespoons all-purpose flour
2 cloves garlic, minced
½ teaspoon dried thyme leaves
¼ teaspoon salt
¼ teaspoon ground nutmeg
¼ teaspoon black pepper
1 package (6 ounces) wheat pilaf mix

1 Preheat oven to 375°F. Cut parchment paper into four 10-inch squares. Place 1 chicken breast in center of each piece of parchment; arrange carrots, zucchini, peas and bell pepper around chicken.

2 Combine ½ cup chicken broth and flour in small saucepan; stir in garlic, thyme, salt, nutmeg and black pepper. Heat to a boil, stirring constantly, until thickened. Reduce heat to low; simmer 1 minute. Spoon broth mixture evenly over chicken and vegetables.

3 Fold each parchment square in half diagonally, enclosing chicken and vegetables to form a triangle. Fold edges over twice to seal. Place parchment packets on 15 × 10-inch jelly-roll pan. Bake 25 to 30 minutes or until parchment is browned and puffed.

4 Place remaining 1¾ cups chicken broth in medium saucepan. Heat to a boil over medium-high heat. Stir in pilaf mix (discard spice packet). Reduce heat to low and simmer, covered, 15 minutes or until broth is absorbed.

5 Arrange parchment packets on serving plates; open carefully. Serve with pilaf.

Makes 4 servings

*Personalized Nutrition Reference for Different Calorie Levels**

Daily Calorie Level	1,600	2,000	2,200	2,800
Total Fat	53 g	65 g	73 g	93 g
% of Calories from Fat	30%	30%	30%	30%
Saturated Fat	18 g	20 g	24 g	31 g
Carbohydrate	240 g	300 g	330 g	420 g
Protein	46 g**	50 g	55 g	70 g
Dietary Fiber	20 g***	25 g	25 g	32 g
Cholesterol	300 mg	300 mg	300 mg	300 mg
Sodium	2,400 mg	2,400 mg	2,400 mg	2,400 mg
Calcium	1,000 mg	1,000 mg	1,000 mg	1,000 mg
Iron	18 mg	18 mg	18 mg	18 mg
Vitamin A	1,000 RE	1,000 RE	1,000 RE	1,000 RE
Vitamin C	60 mg	60 mg	60 mg	60 mg

  *   Numbers may be rounded
 **   46 g is the minimum amount of protein recommended for all
      calorie levels below 1,800.
***   20 g is the minimum amount of fiber recommended for all calorie
      levels below 2,000.

Note: These calorie levels may not apply to children or adolescents, who have varying calorie requirements. For specific advice concerning calorie levels, please consult a registered dietitian, qualified health professional or pediatrician.

Blackened Chicken Salad, 32
Buffalo Chicken Tenders, 16

Californian, The, 12
Cheese Ravioli, 80
Cheese Ravioli with Spinach Pesto and
   Chicken, 78
Chicken and Corn Chowder, 46
Chicken and Couscous Salad, 28
Chicken and Curried Fruit, 76
Chicken and Mozzarella Melts, 24
Chicken and Vegetable Risotto, 60
Chicken and Veggie Lasagna, 67
Chicken Baked in Parchment, 90
Chicken Bourguignonne, 56
Chicken Breasts
   Blackened Chicken Salad, 32
   Californian, The, 12
   Chicken and Corn Chowder, 46
   Chicken and Couscous Salad, 28
   Chicken and Curried Fruit, 76
   Chicken and Mozzarella Melts, 24
   Chicken Baked in Parchment, 90
   Chicken Cordon Bleu, 58
   Chicken, Tortellini and Roasted
      Vegetable Salad, 35
   Crispy Baked Chicken, 86
   Greek-Style Chicken Stew, 48
   Grilled Chicken Breast and
      Peperonata Sandwiches, 14
   Grilled Chicken with Southern
      Barbecue Sauce, 62
   Mediterranean Chicken Kabobs, 84
   Mexican Tortilla Soup, 50
   Pita Pizzas, 22
   Szechuan Chicken Salad, 38
   Tarragon Chicken Salad Sandwiches,
      20
   Tex-Mex Chicken, 70
   Tuscan Chicken Breasts with Polenta,
      81
Chicken Cacciatore, 44
Chicken Cordon Bleu, 58

Chicken Fajitas, 72
Chicken Fricassee, 52
Chicken, Ground
   Chicken and Veggie Lasagna, 67
   Chicken Ravioli Soup, 54
   Meatball Grinders, 26
   White Bean Chili, 42
Chicken Pieces
   Chicken Bourguignonne, 56
   Chicken Cacciatore, 44
   Chicken Fricassee, 52
   Chicken Pot Pie, 74
Chicken Pot Pie, 74
Chicken Ravioli, 54
Chicken Ravioli Soup, 54
Chicken Salad Niçoise, 30
Chicken Tenders
   Buffalo Chicken Tenders, 16
   Cheese Ravioli with Spinach Pesto and
      Chicken, 78
   Chicken and Vegetable Risotto, 60
   Chicken Fajitas, 72
   Chicken Salad Niçoise, 30
   Mediterranean Sandwiches, 18
   Sesame Chicken and Vegetable Stir-
      Fry, 88
Chicken Thighs: Taos Chicken Salad, 40
Chicken, Tortellini and Roasted
   Vegetable Salad, 35
Chicken, Whole: Ricotta Stuffed Chicken
   with Sun-Dried Tomato Linguine,
   64
Crispy Baked Chicken, 86

Entrees, 58–90

Greek-Style Chicken Stew, 48
Grilled Chicken Breast and Peperonata
   Sandwiches, 14
Grilled Chicken with Southern Barbecue
   Sauce, 62

Herb and Mustard Dressing, 30

Lime Vinaigrette, 40

Meatball Grinders, 26
Mediterranean Chicken Kabobs, 84
Mediterranean Sandwiches, 18
Mexican Tortilla Soup, 50

Pita Pizzas, 22

Ranch Salad Dressing, 34
Ricotta Stuffed Chicken with Sun-Dried
   Tomato Linguine, 64

Salad Dressings
   Herb and Mustard Dressing, 30
   Lime Vinaigrette, 40
   Ranch Salad Dressing, 34
   Sun-Dried Tomato and Basil
      Vinaigrette, 36
Salads, 28–40
Sandwiches & Snacks, 12–26
Sauces
   Spinach Pesto, 80
   Tomato-Herb Sauce, 68
   Tuscan Tomato Sauce, 82
Sesame Chicken and Vegetable Stir-Fry,
   88
Soups & Stews, 42–56
Spinach Pesto, 80
Sun-Dried Tomato and Basil Vinaigrette,
   36
Sun-Dried Tomato Linguine, 66
Szechuan Chicken Salad, 38

Taos Chicken Salad, 40
Tarragon Chicken Salad Sandwiches, 20
Tex-Mex Chicken, 70
Tomato-Herb Sauce, 68
Tuscan Chicken Breasts with Polenta,
   81
Tuscan Tomato Sauce, 82

White Bean Chili, 42

VOLUME MEASUREMENTS (dry)

1/8 teaspoon = 0.5 mL
1/4 teaspoon = 1 mL
1/2 teaspoon = 2 mL
3/4 teaspoon = 4 mL
1 teaspoon = 5 mL
1 tablespoon = 15 mL
2 tablespoons = 30 mL
1/4 cup = 60 mL
1/3 cup = 75 mL
1/2 cup = 125 mL
2/3 cup = 150 mL
3/4 cup = 175 mL
1 cup = 250 mL
2 cups = 1 pint = 500 mL
3 cups = 750 mL
4 cups = 1 quart = 1 L

VOLUME MEASUREMENTS (fluid)

1 fluid ounce (2 tablespoons) = 30 mL
4 fluid ounces (1/2 cup) = 125 mL
8 fluid ounces (1 cup) = 250 mL
12 fluid ounces (1 1/2 cups) = 375 mL
16 fluid ounces (2 cups) = 500 mL

WEIGHTS (mass)

1/2 ounce = 15 g
1 ounce = 30 g
3 ounces = 90 g
4 ounces = 120 g
8 ounces = 225 g
10 ounces = 285 g
12 ounces = 360 g
16 ounces = 1 pound = 450 g

DIMENSIONS

1/16 inch = 2 mm
1/8 inch = 3 mm
1/4 inch = 6 mm
1/2 inch = 1.5 cm
3/4 inch = 2 cm
1 inch = 2.5 cm

OVEN TEMPERATURES

250°F = 120°C
275°F = 140°C
300°F = 150°C
325°F = 160°C
350°F = 180°C
375°F = 190°C
400°F = 200°C
425°F = 220°C
450°F = 230°C

BAKING PAN SIZES

Utensil	Size in Inches/Quarts	Metric Volume	Size in Centimeters
Baking or Cake Pan (square or rectangular)	8×8×2	2 L	20×20×5
	9×9×2	2.5 L	22×22×5
	12×8×2	3 L	30×20×5
	13×9×2	3.5 L	33×23×5
Loaf Pan	8×4×3	1.5 L	20×10×7
	9×5×3	2 L	23×13×7
Round Layer Cake Pan	8×1½	1.2 L	20×4
	9×1½	1.5 L	23×4
Pie Plate	8×1¼	750 mL	20×3
	9×1¼	1 L	23×3
Baking Dish or Casserole	1 quart	1 L	—
	1½ quart	1.5 L	—
	2 quart	2 L	—